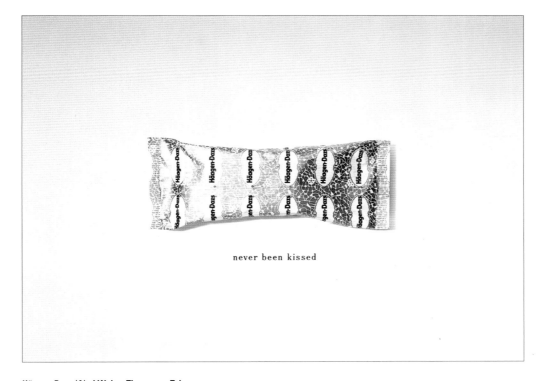

never been kissed

Häagen Dazs (A) J.Walter Thompson, Tokyo
(CD/CW) Eisaku Sekihashi
(AD) Hisa Matsunaga (P) Megumu Wada

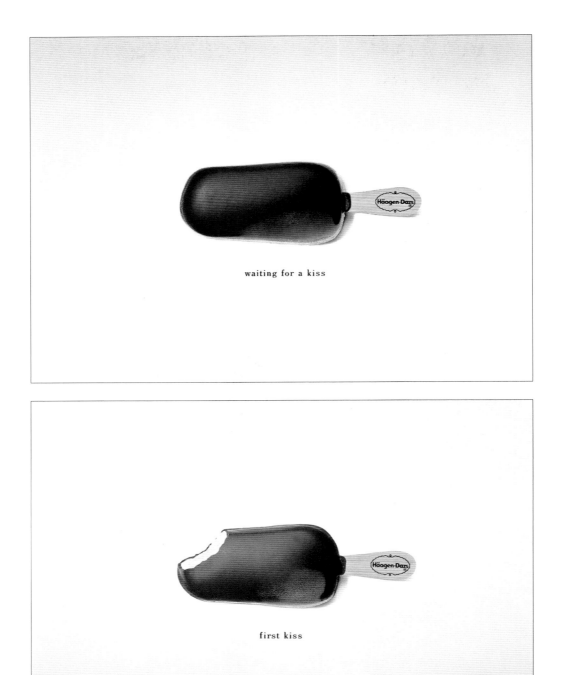

waiting for a kiss

first kiss

BEST ADS FANTASY IN ADVERTISING

Dave Saunders

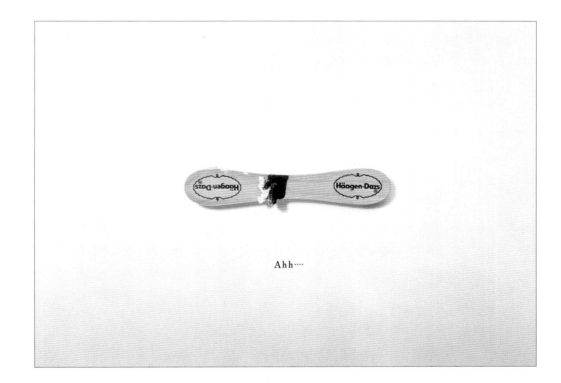

Ahh····

B.T. Batsford Ltd, London

To Fran, who helps turn fantasy into reality

Printed by

for the publishers
B.T.Batsford Ltd
583 Fulham Road
London SW6 5BY

ISBN 0 7134 8104 8

A CIP catalogue record for this book is available from the British Library

(A) Agency, **(CD)** Creative Director, **(AD)** Art Director, **(CW)** Copywriter, **(P)** Photographer, **(M)** Model.

CONTENTS

INTRODUCTION

Anything can happen

Reality imprisons. Fantasy is the key to the highway. All you have to do is to suspend disbelief and be carried out of this world on a journey through the contents of advertising's most creative minds. Anything can happen. And has done with increasing ingenuity since the high-profile surreal ads of the 1960s and 70s. Through the magic of make-believe and the subtlety of symbolism, fantasy in advertising promises the realization of dreams. A bridge between aspiration and attainment. And, after all, without dreams, what hope motivation.

To a degree, all advertising is fantasy. Not that it's untrue. More a case of selective enhanced reality. Visualizing metaphors, inverting logic and inventing new realities are all part of the language of advertising. When talking to a sophisticated, media-literate consumer, imaginative diversion and enigmatic allusion can have greater impact than a sledgehammer. Fantasy highlights a reality. And knowing that it's fantasy doesn't dilute its power. We understand the subtext; we can read between the lines.

Children slip easily into fairy tales, eager to believe that the frog turns into a prince. Fantasies are wonderful. And safe, because they don't bite. We need to reclaim our child-like imaginations …and can do so through the transporting potential of advertising. To recapture lost dreams and revisit Wonderland. Then, when the imagination is released, anything can happen. You might even buy the product.

Smirnoff (A) Young & Rubican, London (AD)
Tony Wheeton (P) Brian Duffy

Fables, Fairy Tales and Fantasies

**Cheltenham & Gloucester Building Society (A) K Advertising, London
(AD/CW) Susie Henry/Judy Smith (P) Michael Portelly**

A 12-year old Israeli boy swims down into an underwater cave
and bursts through a vast shoal of tiny fish to find the pearl
before his heavily-weighted rivals. It's the classic fairy tale of
the small guy - representing versatility and freedom of
movement - outwitting cumbersome, sinister forces. The scene
was shot in Egypt's Ras Mohammed nature reserve.

Bounty Sword (A) Doom, Tokyo
(ADs) Yoshito Kubutoa/Minao Tsukada
(CW) Shoich Kume (P) Hiroshi Nonami
(Stylist/hair/make-up) Yurika Uchida

Once upon a time there were fairy tales.
Our fantasies are realities that don't exist.

Auschem (A) STZ, Milan (AD) Fritz Tschirren
(CW) Marco Ferri (P) Oliviero Toscani

Auschem helps industry make better products.
A kiss of fate transformed Toscani's career from photographer
to prince of polemic. Under Luciano Benetton's benefaction, he
leapfrogged from studio snapper to controversy king.

**Heineken (A) Lowe Howard-Spink, London
(AD) Kevin Jones (CW) Rob Janowsky
(P) Paul Bevitt**

Touchez! Turn the tables by lubricating
your imagination.

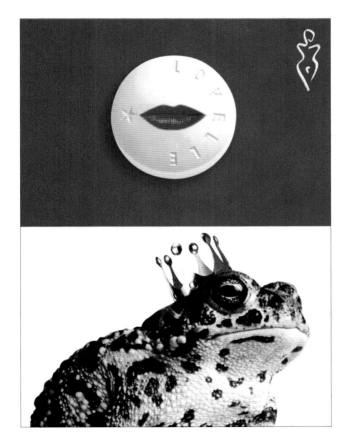

**Organon/Lovelle (A) R.G. Wiesmeier, Munich
(CDs) Gudrun Müllner/Joerg Jahn
(AD) Gudrun Müllner/Martina Schwertlinger
(CW) Joerg Jahn**

With this birth control pill, damsels can
turn toads into princes, instead of
tadpoles into babies.

Heineken refreshes the parts other beers cannot reach.

**Heineken (A) Lowe Howard-Spink, London
(AD) Graham Storey (CW) Phil Cockrell
(P) Malcolm Venville**

The brief was to simulate the costumes
from Coppola's movie Dracula. It is lit from
below to add a sinister touch. A stream of
water was photographed separately, toned
with the colour from a shot of beer, then
stripped in to the main picture twice.

**Beton (A), Springer & Jacoby, Hamberg (CD) Martin Schmidt
(AD) Katja Schumacher (P) Thomas Herbrich**

'Let's hope it's concrete' cries the maiden, with the poetic
licence and dramatic improbability of fairy tales.

**Gallaher, Benson & Hedges (A) Collett Dickenson Pearce,
London (AD) John Merriman (P) Graham Ford**

When the Benson & Hedges surreal campaign first burst onto
the advertising scene, each ad was fantastic - in the real
sense of the word. The campaign propelled the world of
advertising into new realms of fable and fantasy. In order to
avoid creating a predictable pattern, each ad was a surprise.
The only formula was the unpredictability. The wintery
Dickensian shop window was a celebration of one of the most
exciting ad campaigns of the late 1970s and early 1980s.

MIDDLE TAR As defined by H.M. Government
DANGER: Government Health WARNING: CIGARETTES CAN SERIOUSLY DAMAGE YOUR HEALTH.

**Gallaher, Benson & Hedges
(A) Collett Dickenson Pearce,
London (AD) Graham Fink
(P) Ed White**

A suspended carcass of a cow
encouraged the howling wolves
to look up.

BANKS'S MILD ALE

FOLLOW YOUR INSTINCT

**Banks's Mild Ale (A) Woollam
Moira Gaskin O'Malley, London
(CD) Malcolm Gaskin
(P) Bob Carlos Clarke**

Is the image so evocative that
we recall the wolf, then feel
wild about a glass of mild?

これを、待っていた。

…「うまみ」からまる…。

**Master Foods Kal Kan (A) TAI/DMB&B, Tokyo
(CD) Tatsuo Gonda (AD) Akifumi Suzuki
(CW) Hajime Nakamoto**

At last, something worth waking up for. Kal Kan is what cats have been waiting for - in this case, for several hundred years. A maneki neko is a mythical figure of a cat thought to beckon prosperity. The legendary cat resides at Nikko Toshogu, a shrine built in the Edo period (1600-1868) and dedicated to Tokugawa Ieyasu, who established the Tokugawa Shogunate.

My Dream, Your Dream

InterRail (A) Mellors Reay, London (AD) Scott Bain (CW) Gary Dawson (P) Henrik Thorup Knudsen

Freedom to go the way the wind blows - the way the diceman throws - the way you throw your bedclothes.

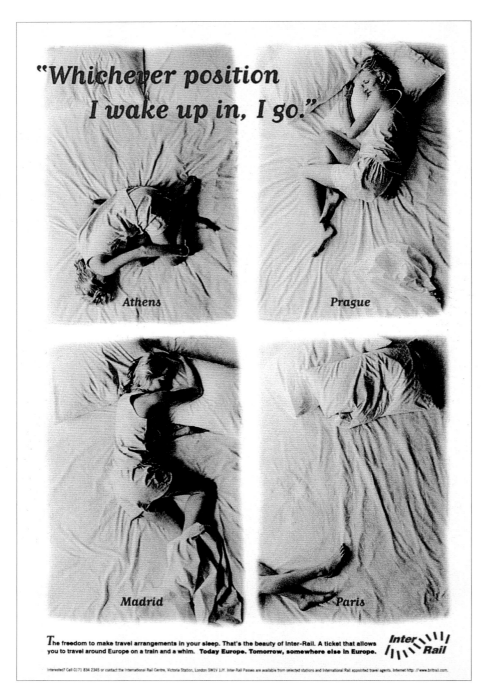

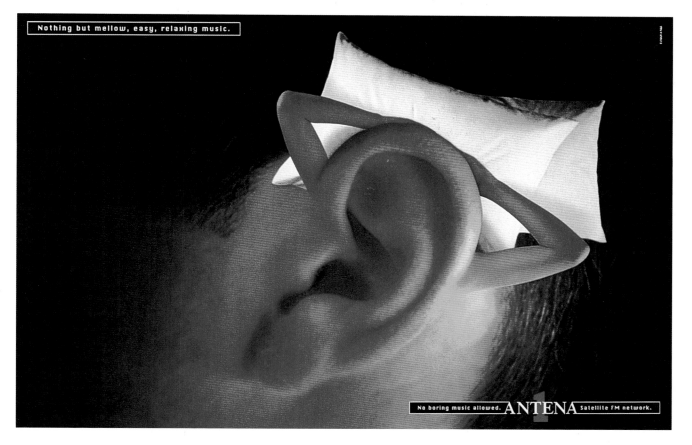

Antena (A) F/Nazca Saatchi & Saatchi, Sao Paulo

Listen and relax. No ear-bending hear.

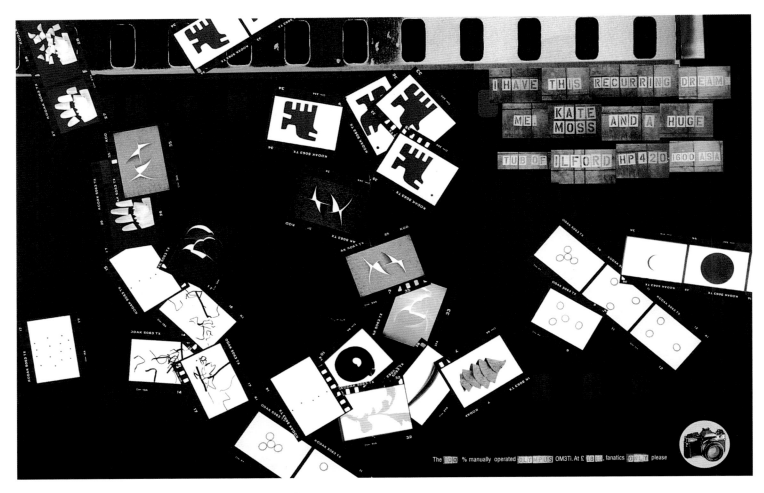

**Olympus Cameras (A) Lowe Howard-Spink, London
(AD) Brian Campbell (CW) Ben Priest (P) Kate Moss**

Your dream may be a little different. The scattered contact
strips point to serious photographers who can afford to shell
out serious money for what has to be a fanatic's camera.

This Secretary's Day why not ask your

handsome, kind-hearted, intelligent,

lovable, genius of a boss

to be so kind as to buy you

a wonderful bottle of perfume like Panache, So..?,

You're the Fire, Royal Secret, Romance, Tweed,

ESP

Tramp, Lace, White Satin or ESP Stayfast.

He is, after all, a gentleman of impeccable taste

and unbounded generosity.

Yardley of London (A) Hunt Lascaris TBWA, Cape Town (CD) Stephen Burke (ADs) Neil Dawson & Grant Parker (CW) Clive Pickering

This tactical ad appeared in the South African press on Secretary's Day, when bosses are encouraged to spoil their secretaries. But knowledge is power. The real translation of the shorthand is: 'You know your lazy, tight-fisted old git of a boss, who's been slave-driving you all year? This Secretary's Day tell him to get off his fat arse, get down to the shops and buy you a wonderful bottle of perfume - such as Panache, So...?, You're the Fire, Royal Secret, Romance, Lace, White Satin, ESP Stayfast, Tweed or Tramp. After everything he's done to get up your nose, it's the least he can do.'

**Linn Products (A) Marr Associates,
Edinburgh (CD/AD) Colin Marr
(CW) Will Taylor**

Ivor Tiefenbrun needed to advertise for a PA. Colin Marr knew that Ivor was no ordinary man. So no ordinary PA would be up to the job. Hence the ads. Subsequently, Mr Tiefenbrun conducted the interviews in the woodland around the Linn factory, while sitting in his underpants at a picnic table.

Dr Jekyll seeks P.A.

MEET Ivor Tiefenbrun, the Managing Director of Linn Products. A Company whose reputation is built firmly on the production of some of the world's finest hi-fi equipment. Since his last P.A. rose to stardom within the Company, the position is vacant once again.

Ivor is a man with a full day. Every day. Though he's just as happy making the time to recall anecdotes to staff as he is revolutionising the hi-fi industry. (Something he tends to do with almost monotonous regularity.) He's refreshingly devoid of stereotypical managerial traits and respects what you do more than what you are. He positively encourages initiative and always has an open ear to a good idea.

But it is his singular charm that not only makes him delightful company but also Linn's biggest P.R. asset. This is a man who's won awards for being nice. (The hi-fi industry recently voted him "Personality of the Year".)

In short, he's a big hearted fellow with an unerring passion for his work.

So, what kind of P.A. does he want?

Ideally, you're perfectly happy in your current job as an executive P.A. with a major international company.

You're aged over 25 and possess impeccable secretarial skills. Linn currently have dealings with over 35 countries around the globe so you should have the kind of lifestyle that can accommodate short notice foreign travel. It's also an opportunity for you to brush up on any foreign languages you may have.

The first stage is to send a one page C.V. to Ivor Tiefenbrun at the address below.

Linn Products Ltd, Floors Road,
Waterfoot, Eaglesham, Glasgow G76 0EP.

Mr Hyde seeks P.A.

MEET Ivor Tiefenbrun, the Managing Director of Linn Products who "make the best hi-fi in the world."*

He wants a new P.A.

Ivor is a man with a full day. Every day. Though that can mean anything from disappearing from his desk without a trace to wandering around with a pig-headed arrogance that is as irksome as it is distracting. (Something he does with almost monotonous regularity.) To say that he was tiresome would be an understatement. He's a petulant, narrow-minded man who appears to have little respect for the people who suffer his managerial reign. He is convinced that Ivor Tiefenbrun has the only worthwhile opinion and rarely takes counsel or listens to advice.

But perhaps Ivor's most interesting characteristic is his public face. (Not a pretty sight.) He doesn't think twice about giving members of the hi-fi press a frank appraisal of their competence. "Human debris" being just one from a long and colourful list of his conclusions. The result is that the M.D. of Linn Products neatly doubles up as their worst P.R. nightmare.

In short, this is a man with a monstrous personality problem.

So, what kind of P.A. does he need?

Well, you're not the type of person who takes things too personally. As the closest person to Ivor, you'll take the brunt of his offensive behaviour. You should be strong minded and possess a natural diplomacy that can cover the messiest of Ivor's tracks. (Press conferences being a notable example.)

You have a constitution of steel, are personable and intelligent. You should also be able to concentrate on getting a job done when everyone else seems intent on making it impossible.

If this proposition in any way attracts you then you should firstly contact a psychiatrist and then promptly send a one page C.V. to the address below.

* Ivor Tiefenbrun

Linn Products Ltd, Floors Road,
Waterfoot, Eaglesham, Glasgow G76 0EP.

**Prudential Insurance (A) Fallon McElligott, Minneapolis
(AD) Amy Nicholson (CW) Bill Westbrook (P) Jose Picayo**

Become involved with real people's dreams, and you begin to
care for them. By sifting through their mind and sharing their
hopes and plans, you identify their footsteps. And from there,
you identify with the path they follow.

Live well.
*"I'm an inveterate optimist. And I hate people who are not optimistic
around me. The ones who try to clip your wings, you know?"*

Make a plan.
*"I think the greatest thing about living is the gift of
managing your life to make the best of it. I don't understand people
who say, 'Live one day at a time.'"*

Be your own rock.
*Prudential offers life insurance, investments, health coverage and
real estate that can help you manage your life. And live well.*

The**Prudential**

FIRETRAP

AUTUMN/WINTER

as exciting as what's on your mind.

**Firetrap (A) M & C Saatchi, London
(AD) Gary Marshall (CW) Paul Marshall**

A trendy clothing company wanted to
produce some sparky fashion ads. The
style of illustration adds to the funkiness.

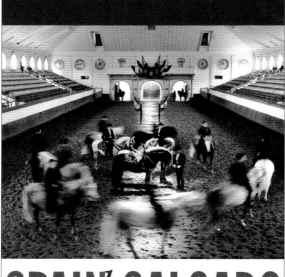

Spanish Tourist Board (A) Delvico Bates, Madrid (CDs) Pedro Soler/Enrique Astuy (AD) Peter Rose (P) Michael Kenna, Jean Baptiste Mondino, Sebastião Salgado Magnum, Javier Vallhonrat

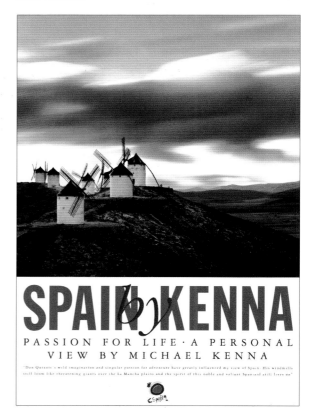

This image-building campaign gave eleven of the world's leading photographers free rein to produce personal pictures of Spain. In some cases the reins were tightened a little in order to keep the artistic visions within the pragmatic aims of the client. By art-directing photographers of this calibre, you are in danger of limiting them to the boundaries of your imagination.

Act Laterally

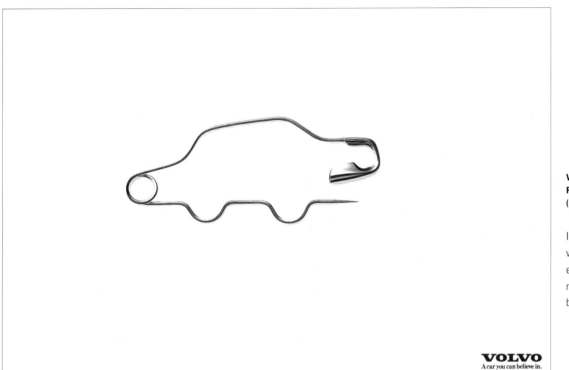

Volvo Cars Japan (A) Dentsu, Young & Rubicam, Tokyo (AD) Masakazu Sawa (CW) Minoru Kawase (P) Megumu Wada

Involuntarily, your brain whispers the words, and the symbolism is instantly etched on your memory. Following the newspaper campaign, sales increased by 20%.

VOLVO
A car you can believe in.

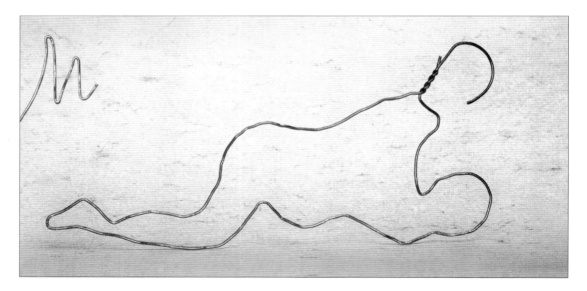

Mates Condoms (A) Knight Leach Delaney, London (AD) Andy Wray (CW) Paul Delaney (P) Steve Thompson

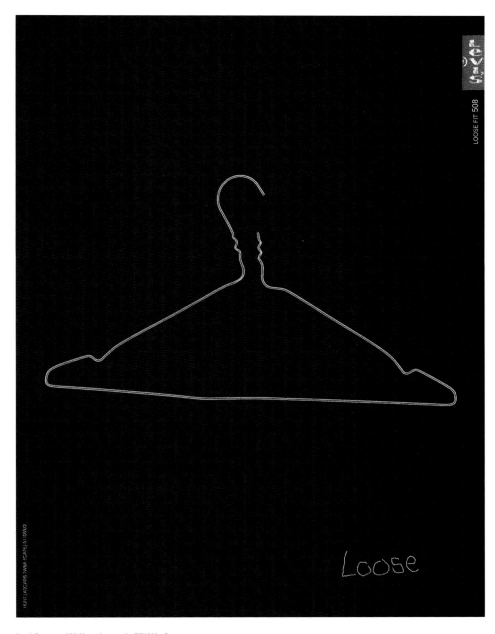

Levi Strauss (A) Hunt Lascaris TBWA, Cape
Town (CD) Stephen Burke (AD) Grant Parker

Fortis (A) TBWA/Campaign Company, Amsterdam (ADs) Béla Stamenkovits & Paul Rietveld (CW) Rob Floor (P) Hans Kroeskamp

There is strength in numbers. Together, we can catch the prize.

Shore's Lures (A) BVK/McDonald, Milwaukee
(AD) Scott Krahn (CW) Gary Mueller (P) Dick Baker

They are so irresistibly scrummy, the fish
don't stand a chance.

Gallaher/Silk Cut (A) Saatchi & Saatchi, London
(CD) Paul Arden (AD) Alexandra Taylor (CWs) John Messum
& Paul Atkins (P) Umberto Rivas (Modelmaker) Shirtsleeves

**7mg TAR 0·7mg NICOTINE
SMOKING CAUSES FATAL DISEASES
Health Departments' Chief Medical Officers**

Given the words 'purple silk' and 'cut', how many interpretations can there be? When the campaign was first launched in 1983, it was difficult to see how it could move on from the simple torn material. But by fanning out from the core concept, it seems that this scenario could run and run.

7mg TAR 0·7mg NICOTINE
SMOKING KILLS
Health Departments' Chief Medical Officers

**Gallaher/Silk Cut (A) Saatchi & Saatchi, London
(CDs) Paul Arden & Alexandra Taylor (AD) Carlos
(CW) Steve Bickel (P) François Gillet**

This campaign will dance to any tune it can can.

Friends of the Earth (A) McCann Erickson, London (AD/CW) Simon Hepton/Matt Crabtree (P) Andy Atkinson

Another global warning from our collective conscience.

THERE'S NOT ALWAYS A GOV

Join now 01:

FRIENDS *of the* **earth**

NMENT HEALTH WARNING.

2 297

SMOKING CAUSES CANCER
Chief Medical Officers' Warning
12 mg Tar 0.9 mg Nicotine

**Gallaher/Benson & Hedges (A) Collett Dickenson Pearce, London
(AD) Nigel Rose (P) Graham Ford**

The Midas touch caught Tabs fishing for gold. The cardboard
cutout was photographed completely in-camera.

**Kodak (A) J. Walter Thompson, Tokyo
(AD) Junichiro Morita (CW) Eisaku Sekihashi
(P) Tetsuro Takai**

What's next? The client wanted to use new modes of expression to demonstrate how Kodak film is pushing forward the frontiers of image making.

Tesco Stores (A) Lowe Howard-Spink, London
(AD) Alan Davis (CW) Jez Willy (P) Elliott Erwitt/Magnum

Ah yes, that reminds me...

United Distillers/Dewar's White Label (A) Casadevall Pedréno & PRG, Barcelona (AD/CW) Pepino García (Ps) Shu Akashi/Rafael Jover

Turn conventional wisdom on its head and celebrate the fact that it's not your birthday. Today is not a milestone which highlights your increasing age.

Dewar's (A) Leo Burnett, Chicago

Hey! Just what kind of a man are you? Man
of the world? Can handle yourself? Prove it.

Jim Beam (A) Fallon McElligott, Minneapolis (AD) Deb Hagan (CW) Bill Westbrook (P) Guzman

We can choose to allow our self image to be enhanced or altered by the personality of products. The feelgood factor comes in many shades - feeling tough, sexy, successful, desireable - any one of which can be tapped into by advertisers.

Get in touch with your masculine side.

Swish Jeans (A) Saatchi & Saatchi, Rome (CD) Stephano Maria
Palombi/Luca Albanese (AD) Grazia Cecconi (CW) Stephano Maria
Palombi (Ps) Mark Liddel/Ottavio Celestino

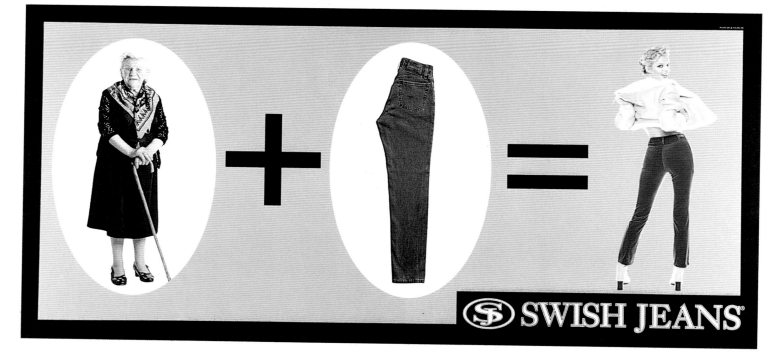

Levi's jeans modelled
by original wearer.
Model : Josephine, 79, teacher, Colorado.
Item : 534 women's fit jeans.
Stylist : Simon Foxton.
Hair : Kevin Ryan.
Photographer : Nick Knight.

**Levi Strauss/Red Tab (A) Bartle Bogle Hegarty, London
(CD) John Hegarty (AD) Steve Hudson (CW) Victoria Fallon
(P) Nick Knight**

Check list: is this right for the brand? Will it startle? Is
it original? And does it make the hairs on the back of
your neck stand up?

He complimented you on your perfume. You weren't wearing any.

Lee

The Brand That Fits.

Lee Jeans (A) Fallon McElligott, Minneapolis
(AD) Harvey Marco (CW) Nancy Nelms (P) Moshe Brakha

How many different ways can you avoid simply saying
'These are great jeans. Buy them'?

Makes me feel good. Hugs me. Flatters me. (Shame it's only a bra.)

The bra for the way you are.

**Triumph International (A) Delaney Fletcher Bozell, London
(CDs) Greg Delaney/Brian Stewart (AD) Brian Stewart
(CW) Greg Delaney (P) Pamela Hanson, represented by Fiona
Cowan/Hamiltons Photographers Ltd.**

The tone is light, human, real life, without being too risqué.

UNITED COLORS
OF BENETTON.

Benetton (A) In-house, Italy (AD/P) Oliviero Toscani

A fantasy expressing the desire for a more equitable reality.
Shame it's only advertising clothes.

**Asprey (A) M & C Saatchi, London
(AD) Gary Marshall (CW) Paul Marshall
(P) Helmut Newton, represented by Tiggy
Maconochie/Hamiltons Photographers Ltd.**

The jewellery and luxury goods store
re-dresses its staid image to lure the
hip offspring of its traditional clients.
Or is it just a good old-fashioned
wealth fantasy?

Aadvarks With Sunglasses

Jonathan Sceats Sunglasses
(A) BAM/SSB, Sydney (AD) Darryn Devlin
(CW) Bobbi Gassy (P) Michael Corridore

Re-interpreting a phrase with a literal
visual is a well-worn - and arresting -
advertising solution. The macabre
treatment targets the cynical and
fashion-conscious 18-30 irreverent end
of the market, that wouldn't be seen
dead in anything else.

Zoomp (A) F/Nazca Saatchi & Saatchi, Sao Paulo (AD) Eduardo Martins (CW) João Livi (P) Fernando Zuffo

I love frogs. They are much more amusing than people. Not to mention crazier and cuter. And they don't work 12 hours a day just to make it to the cover of *Forbes* one day. Not forgetting the fact that it takes just one kiss to turn one of them into a prince. Or at least into an amorous frog.

Gallaher/Benson & Hedges (A) Collett Dickenson Pearce, London (AD) Guy Moore (CW) Tony Malcolm (P) Nick Georghiou and stock

As soon as you understand the visual clues of a campaign, you can share the joke. In this reconstruction of J.R. Eyerman's 3-D movie image, gold is the key to enlightenment.

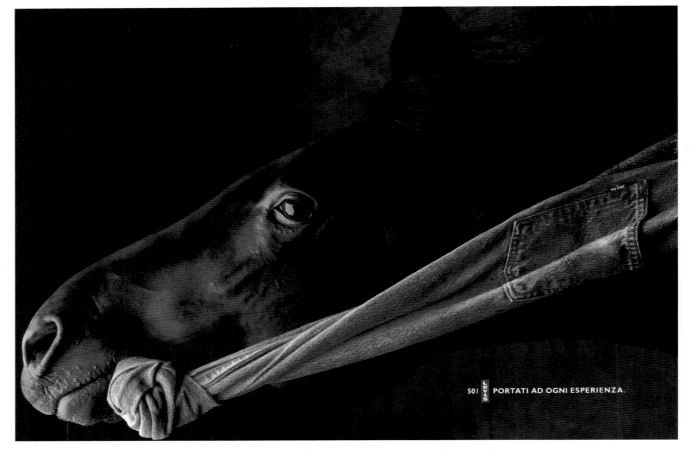

Levi Strauss (A) McCann Erickson, Milan (AD) Stefano Colombo
(CW) Alessandro Canale (P) Graham Ford

The red tab on the 'reins' is legible only because the 6x6 photo finish
was shot inside the stable. The copyline 'Fit for whatever' works as
well in Italian as in English.

Gallaher/Benson & Hedges (A) Jung
von Matt, Hamburg (CD) Stefan
Zschaler (AD) Ove Gley (CW) Oliver
Kessler (P) Uwe Düttmann

For a really good cigarette, you can
advertise with almost anything.

**Perrier Vittel UK (A) Publicis, London (AD) Rick Ward
(CW) Noel Sharman (P) Paul Bevitt (Modelmaker) Tim Weare & Partners**

Three executions of the campaign appeared in London in the
summer of 1995. They were the best liked posters of the season
and also increased sales significantly.

"DO WHAT U CAN, WITH WHAT U HAVE, WHERE U R." - THEODORE ROOSEVELT

REEBOKS LET U.B.U.

Reebok (A) Chiat Day, New York (AD) Marty Cooke

Goggles, sox and Reeboks. Be yourself. Free
yourself. Whatever you want!

**Bluna (A) Jung von Matt, Hamburg
(CDs) Stefan Zschaler & Ove Gley
(AD) Thomas Pakull (CW) Bernard Lukas
(P) Stefan Försterling/Frederick J. Phillips**

Aren't we all a little Bluna? The ad adds
meaning and character to the product,
as well as coining a new word.

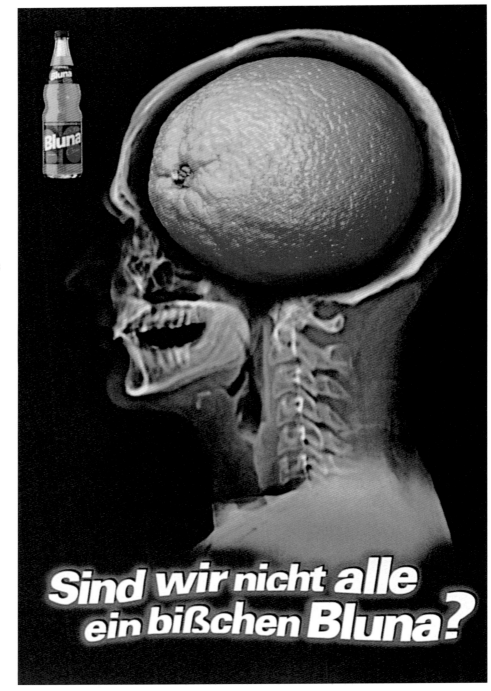

Smirnoff (A) Lowe Howard-Spink, London (AD) Alan Davis
(CW) Jez Willy (P) Malcolm Venville

Swatch (A) Barbella Gagliardi Saffirio,
Milan (CD) Pasquale Barbella
(AD) Manuela Colombo (CW) Laura Colombo
(P) Hermes Carli

Ever since the marketing people realised
that watches are now cheap enough to
become a fun accessory, zany designs
have flourished. Unless you look on the
sunny side, the yoke's on you.

Rover Equinox (A) Ammirati Puris Lintas, London (CD) Andrew Cracknell (AD) Melanie Forster (CW) Michelle Stewart (P) Frank Herholdt (M) Valentina Contato of Elite/Premier

The Mini Special Edition is launched in the fashion press in a stylized couture pastiche of a Mini dress.

Flesh and Fantasies

Levi Strauss (A) Catchline, Amsterdam
(AD) Wim de Boer (CW) Hans Neerhout
(P) Dieter Eikelpoth

Some great feelings last for seconds...

...some for years.

LEVI'S

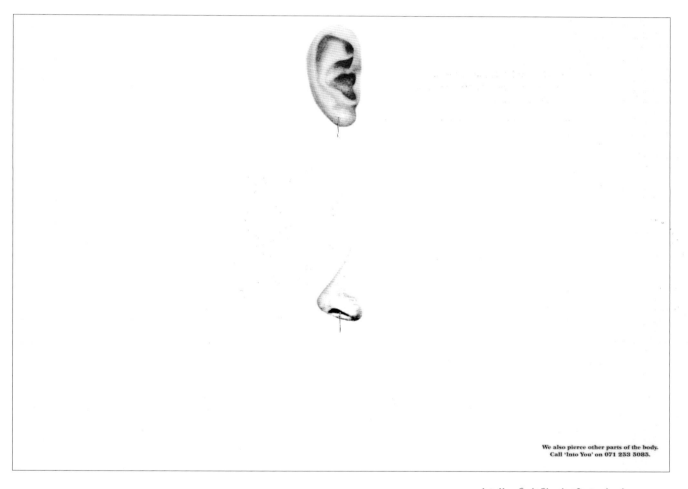

We also pierce other parts of the body.
Call 'Into You' on 071 253 5085.

**Into Your Body Piercing Centre, London
(AD) Scott Bain (CW) Gary Dawson**

Mates Condoms (A) Knight Leach Delaney,
London (AD) Andy Wray (CW) Paul Delaney
(P) Martin Thompson

If you're looking for the real thing, look twice.

Avoid imitations.
Buy your Levi's jeans only from Original Levi's Stores and Authorised Dealers.

Levi Strauss (A) Bassat Ogilvy & Mather,
Barcelona (AD) Alex Lazaro (CW) Gustavo
Caldas (P) Mike Diver (M) D'Arcy Drag Queen

Zita Fabiani (A) STZ, Milan
(CD/AD/CW) Fritz Tschirren/ Marco Ferri
(P) Andrea Pizzi

Clothes men like ... so much they can
become quite attached to them.

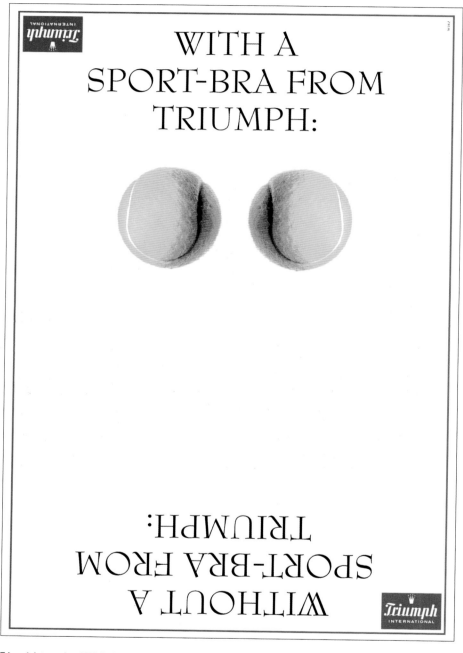

Triumph International/Tri-Action Sport-BH
(A) Wirz Werbeberatung, Zurich
(CD/CW) André Benker (AD) Danielle Lanz
(P) Felix Streuli

SMOKING CAUSES FATAL DISEASES

Chief Medical   Officers' Warning
5 mg Tar   0.5 mg Nicotine

Gallaher/Silk Cut (A) M & C Saatchi, London
(AD) Martin Casson (CW) Nick Drummond (P) Donna Trope

A spiky alternative to cigarette ads claiming a
cool smooth taste.

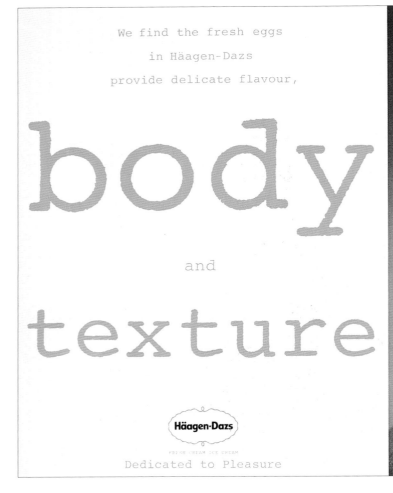

We find the fresh eggs
in Häagen-Dazs
provide delicate flavour,

body

and

texture

Häagen·Dazs

FRESH CREAM ICE CREAM

Dedicated to Pleasure

Häagen Dazs (A) Bartle Bogle Hegarty, London (CD) John Hegarty (AD) Rooney Carruthers (CW) Larry Barker (P) Jeanloup Sieff, represented by Tiggy Maconochie/Hamiltons Photographers Ltd

Stimulating a rich and creamy flow of controversy and spoofs, early Häagen Dazs ads oozed fleshy fantasy.

Smirnoff (A) Lowe Howard-Spink, London
(CD) Paul Weinberger (AD) Jeff Curtis
(CW) Adrian Lim (P) Sheila Metzner

Nightmares

United Distillers XLR8 (A) Leo Burnett Connaghan and May, Sydney (AD) Andy Iles (CW) Dave Shirlaw

The brand name for this new alcoholic cola was invented by the ad agency to convey the racy pace of constant change. The aim was to win street cred among the 24-plus inner city drinkers.

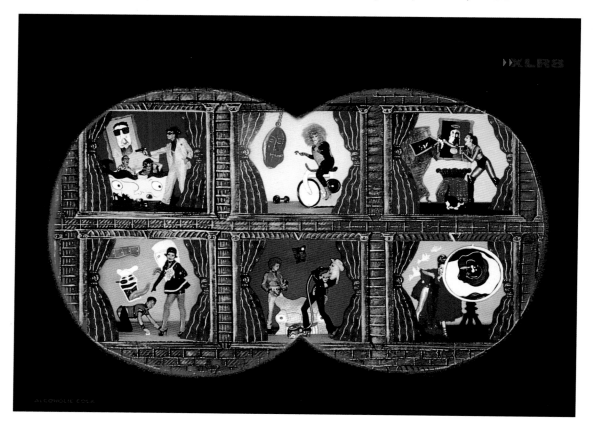

once upon a time there was a girl named Wendy who was very beautiful and very happy and had lots of friends but then one day she did some heroin and got addicted and lost everything and then she died.

The End.

Life on heroin is no fairy tale.
Before you start using heroin, think about how hard it is to stop.
PARTNERSHIP FOR A DRUG-FREE AMERICA®

Partnership for a Drug-free America (A) Hill Holliday Connors Cosmopulos, Boston (CD) Fred Bertino (AD) Wendy Lewis (CW) Baxter Taylor (P) Matt Mahurin

Once upon a time there was a girl named Wendy. I wonder where the art director got that name from. Every moral fairy tale has a sad ending. For someone. Life on heroin is no fairy tale. A trip into this fantasy ends up in a darker, distorted reality.

Benetton (A) In-house, Italy (AD) Oliviero Toscani

Critics view the Benetton ads themselves as more of a nightmare than the issues they address. The Aids seen in these 1000 faces is not always as visible.

Levi Strauss (A) Bassat Ogilvy & Mather,
Barcelona (ADs) David Ruiz & Alex Lazaro
(CW) Gustavo Caldes (P) Ricardo Miras &
Horillo Riola

Golden Wonder (A) Bartle Bogle Hegarty, London (CD) Dennis Lewis
(AD) Andrew Smart (CW) Roger Beckett (P) Mark Polyblank
(Modelmaker) Tim Weare & Partners (Typographer) Andy Bird

Swatch (A) Barbella Gagliardi Saffirio, Milan
(CD) Pasquale Barbella (ADs) Paolo Rutigliano &
Roberto Badò (CWs) Roberta Sollazzi & Roberto Badò
(P) Coppi & Barbieri (Illustrator) Roberto Molino

**Gallaher/Silk Cut (A) M & C Saatchi, London
(CD) James Lowther (AD) Martin Casson
(CW) Nick Drummond (P) Tony May**

The sense of foreboding is a departure
from the usual light and cheery
interpretation of the 'purple silk' and
'cut' theme. Blameless bagpipes are
brought to life, only to face the danger
of becoming entrapped.

SMOKING CAUSI

Chief Medica

5mg Tar

FATAL DISEASES

cers' Warning
g Nicotine

SMOKING KILLS

Chief Medical Officers' Warning
5 mg Tar   0.5 mg Nicotine

**Gallaher/Silk Cut (A) M & C Saatchi, London (CD) James Lowther
(AD) Martin Casson (CW) Nick Drummond (P) Simon Somerville,
represented by Andrea Rosenberg (Modelmaker) Facto**

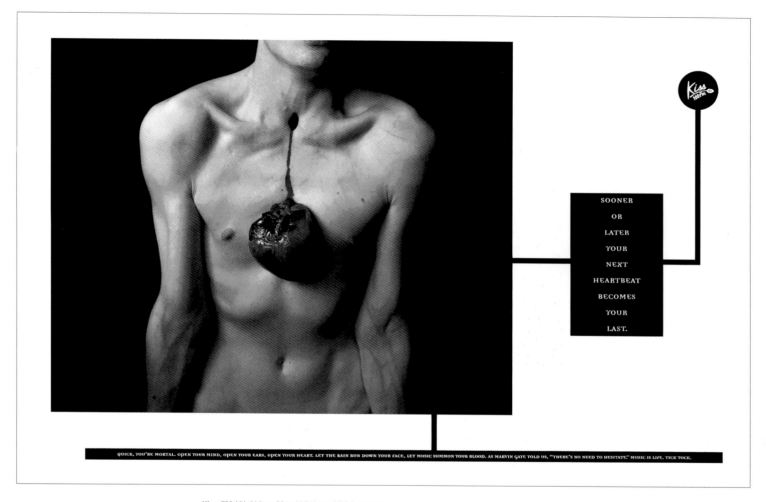

SOONER
OR
LATER
YOUR
NEXT
HEARTBEAT
BECOMES
YOUR
LAST.

QUICK, YOU'RE MORTAL. OPEN YOUR MIND, OPEN YOUR EARS, OPEN YOUR HEART. LET THE RAIN RUN DOWN YOUR FACE, LET MUSIC SUMMON YOUR BLOOD. AS MARVIN GAYE TOLD US, "THERE'S NO NEED TO HESITATE." MUSIC IS LIFE. TICK TOCK.

**Kiss FM (A) Abbott Mead Vickers BBDO, London
(AD) Walter Campbell (CW) Tom Carty (P) Cindy Palmano**

Your next heartbeat. The tension between the heart-stopping image
and the vibrant, pulsing copy insists you pay attention and listen.

The Great Escape

Asda free-range eggs.
Laid by free-range hens.

ASDA

You'd be off your trolley to go anywhere else.

Associated Dairies (A) Bartle Bogle Hegarty, London (AD) Mark Denton (CW) Chris Palmer (P) Stak Aivaliotis

The supermarket chain wanted to put across an image of quality while also being fun, and in touch with its customers. When promoting free-range eggs on posters, the agency chose to use models rather than cartoons, in order to retain the sense of quality. The mundane subject of eggs was enlivened through a McQueen-esque escape involving the hen's flight to freedom from Colditz-like incarceration.

**Cockspur (A) Burkitt Weinrich Bryant, London
(AD) Paul Simblett (P) Nick Georghiou**

Escaping doesn't have to mean going somewhere else.

Rowntree Kit Kat (A) J. Walter Thompson, London
(AD) Steve Mawhinney (P) Nadav Kandar

**Have a break.
Have a cat.**

(Jaguar für 199,-/Tag)

Sixt hat die Katze für wenig Mäuse. Für den Jaguar Sovereign zahlen Sie nur 199,-/Tag. Und sammeln dabei 500 Lufthansa Meilen. Tel.: 0180/521 41 41.

Sixt Autovermietung **Budget** rent a car

**Sixt GmbH & Co (A) Jung von Matt, Hamburg (CD) Jean-Remy von Matt
(AD) Bärbel Biwald (CW) Oliver Voss (P) Andreas Burz**

The tag line for the global Kit Kat campaign provides an
engagingly appropriate word play. Almost every single animal's
name has now been registered as a trade mark - including Jaguar.

Importaciones y Exportaciones Varma/Cutty Sark (A) Delvico Bates, Madrid (CDs) Pedro Soler/Enrique Astuy (AD/CW) Angel Villalba/Jorge Herrera/Sandra Garcia (P) Stock (pyramids)/Carlos Navajas (sunflowers)

Escape. Be an individual. The colour yellow is synonymous with distinctiveness, originality, freedom and escape. Pretty attractive qualities to link to your brand. The ads target a young, intelligent audience, saying 'Don't feel sad and grey ... follow the yellow!'

**Louis Vuitton (A) Creative Business RSCG, Paris
(AD) Jean-François Bentz (P) Jean Larivière**

Trunks, suitcases, bags, two attractive models and a few
jouets were taken to Patagonia to recreate an expensive fantasy.
The result was evocative, nostalgic, yet minimalistic.

**Wildrift (A) Contract Advertising, New Delhi
(AD) Bhupesh Luther (CW) Vidur Vohra
(P) Gaurav Bharadwaj**

Conceived, designed and executed by an
Indian ad agency, the ads feel more
exotic and remote than many wild and
rustic ads crafted by European or
American creatives.

No blossoming
schoolgirls, no debutantes
in clinging clothes,
**no attractive
older women.** Not
much in the way of
excitement and adventure.

No parading
up and down the mall,
**no May Queen
ball**, what's a
girl supposed to do?

See "GoldenEye" and see the BMW that made James Bond switch. THE ULTIMATE DRIVING MACHINE.

**BMW (A) Fallon McElligott, Minneapolis (AD) Bill Schwab
(CW) Joel Lovering (P) Vic Huber**

Energize the James Bond in you. Join the secret agent in the
forefront of technology, and gently reject its classic forerunner.

FROM TIME to time, everyone feels like they want to get away from it all. Now, if you drive a Jeep Cherokee, you don't have to rely on your imagination to transport you there. Thanks to the Command-trac or optional Select-trac full-time four-wheel drive systems you can reach the destinations of even your wildest dreams. The Jeep Cherokee is available in a range of engine sizes, including the nifty 2.5L Turbo Diesel or petrol versions and a power-packed 4.0L petrol, for when you want to make a quick getaway. The Quadra-link suspension system will give you a smooth ride, no matter how rough the terrain. Uni-frame construction, driver's side air bag, power-assisted steering side-impact protection bars and optional four wheel ABS, means the Jeep Cherokee is equipped to ensure you return home safely. And with more and more cars on (and off) the road, the classic Jeep design, with its distinctive crisp, clean lines means you'll never get lost in the crowd. Call 0800 XXXXXX and we'll give you directions on how to get to your nearest Jeep Cherokee showroom. Well, we don't want you getting lost, do we?

Jeep
The American Legend.

Chrysler Jeep Cherokee (A) Delaney Fletcher Bozell, London
(AD) Brian Stewart (CW) Greg Delaney (P) Michael Kenna

With this vehicle you don't have to rely on your
imagination to take you away from it all.

Chrysler Jeep (A) Bozell, Southfield, Michigan

No, this isn't escapism. My Jeep is!

Virtual Fantasies

Nao Xuan Hao of the Tien Giang Province is bowled over by the 1995 Frontera's torquey new engine and improved ground clearance. Se a different world THE 1995 FRONTERA FROM VAUXHALL

Vauxhall Frontera (A) Lowe Howard-Spink, London (AD) Charles Inge (CW) Phil Dearman (P) Andy Green

A fisherman on Lake Tanganyika catches sight of the 1995 Frontera demonstrating its powerful new engine and up-rated coil suspension. Se a different world THE 1995 FRONTERA FROM VAUXHALL

**Singapore Airlines Cargo (A) Ogilvy &
Mather, Singapore (AD) Thomas Low
(CW) Steve Elrick (P) Thomas Herbrich**

We can take cargo anywhere, and make
it happen.

NOW ANYONE CAN LOOK LIKE McENROE.

**Nike (A) Grierson Craig Cockman Daviff (AD) Linda Kitchen
(CW) Dave Daviff (P) Michael Joseph**

Anyone could look like this - with the right gear. Even a
poodle. You can't be serious. All the models - except one -
were non-professionals, recruited from 150 responses to a
single ad in a Sunday paper

TagHeuer (A) BDDP, Paris (AD) Eric Holden (CW) Rémy Noel (P) Guzman (hurdle), Nadav Kander (gymnast)

It's about precision. Focusing the mind. Mistakes can be costly.

Kronenborg 1664 (A) BDDP, Paris
(AD) Philippe Taroux (CW) Benoît Leroux
(P) Guzman

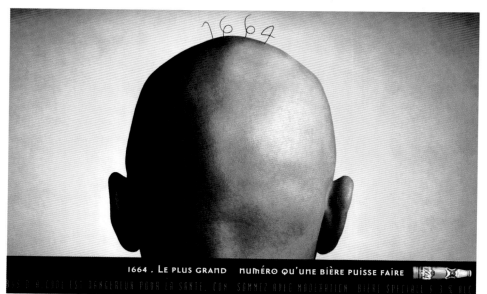

Where do you find vast wheat fields with perfect water-skiing?

Europe. One place more than ever, but still home to an incredible diversity of lifestyles and cultures. And, as a company that has grown from this diversity, Shell sees it as an opportunity, not an obstacle. In the wheat fields of Northern Germany, for example, a herbicide developed by Shell helps maintain the yield of the summer harvest. Meanwhile, in the Greek Islands, tourists' speedboats no longer foul the seawater thanks to Shell's new biodegradable marine engine oil. Small things, perhaps, to a big corporation. But not to a local company. A company like Shell.

Shell (A) Bartle Bogle Hegarty, London (P) Graham Westmoreland

An eye-catching, but convoluted way of saying the company is eco-friendly. In the wheatfields of Northern Germany, a herbicide developed by Shell helps maintain yields. Meanwhile, in the Greek islands, their biodegradable marine engine oil helps minimize pollution from speedboats.

Pirelli Motorcycle Tyres (A) Young & Rubicam, London
(AD) Graeme Norways (CW) Leighton Ballett (P) Albert Watson

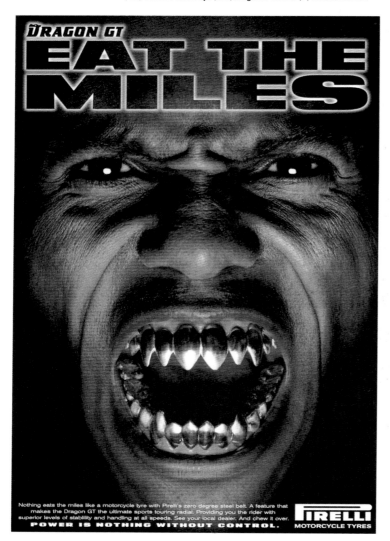

**International Wool Secretariat (A) Abbott Mead
Vickers BBDO, London (AD) Peter Gausis
(CW) Alfredo Marcantonio (P) Nadav Kander**

Face value. Things are not always as they seem.

VIENT LE MOMENT OÙ TOUT PLAIDE EN FAVEUR D'UNE VOLVO.

Volvo Switzerland (A) Aebi Strebel, Zurich (AD) Rene Sennhauser
(P) David Stewart

The name Volvo is derived from the Latin volvo, meaning to
roll. If this ad was not a success, presumably heads would roll.

Fantasy and Reality

**Smirnoff (A) Lowe Howard-Spink, London (AD) Colin Lamberton
(CW) Seyoan Vela (P) Andreas Heumann**

Vladimir Smirnoff fled the Russian Revolution and built a
vodka distillery in Paris in the 1920s. The brand is now valued
at more than $1 billion.

WHAT the HEAL'S going ON ?

Furniture Lighting Fabrics China Glass Gifts Bedlinen Kitchens

TOTTENHAM CT RD. W1 & TUNSGATE GUILDFORD

Heal's (A) Leagus Shafron Davis Ayer, London (AD) Mark Reddy (CW) Richard Grisdale (P) David Stewart

In subsequent ads the blatant pun is replaced by a simple question mark in place of the apostrophe.

Habitat (A) Saatchi & Saatchi, London (AD) Anthony Easton (CW) Adam Kean (P) Andrew MacPherson

Some ads are memorable simply because they are quirky. There's something acceptably surreal about not having to find explanations for everything.

Discover the tribal influences behind Habitat's new autumn collection. (Mrs. Livingroom, I presume?)

Nikon (A) Fallon McElligott, Minneapolis (AD) Sean Robertson (CW) Rob McPherson (P) Matthew Rolston

Many ads make believe you can turn fantasies into reality with their products or services. Some can.

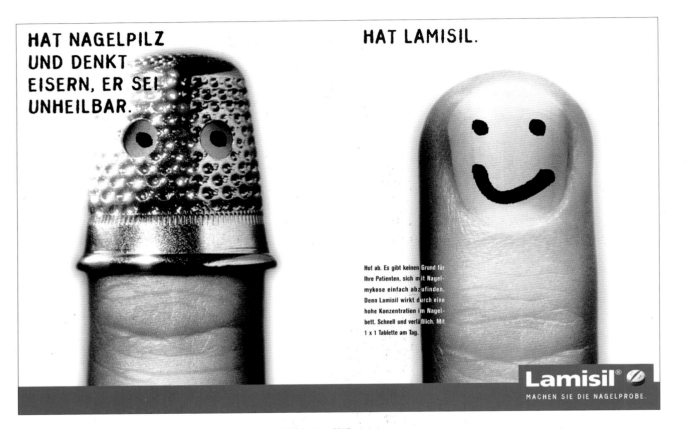

**Sandoz Lamisil (A) R.G. Wiesmeier, Munich (CD) Gudrum Müllner
(CD/CW) Hajo Depper (AD) Martina Schwertlinger (P) Hubertus Hamm**

Hats off to sufferers of mycosis of the nail who take one tablet
of Lamisil a day.

POWER

CLASSIC *f*M 100-102

Classic FM (A) BST.BDDP, London
(CD) Tom Hudson (AD) Brian Connolly
(CW) Steve Hough (P) Nadav Kander

Music can transform your outlook.
A selection of musical instruments
creates new realities.

EXHILARATION

CLASSIC *f*M 100-102

PROTECT CHILDREN: DON'T MAKE THEM BREATHE YOUR SMOKE

Chief Medical   Officers' Warning
5 mg Tar   0.5 mg Nicotine

Gallaher/Silk Cut (A) M & C Saatchi, London
(ADs) Louis Bogue/Carlos (CW) Pete Cain
(P) The Douglas Brothers (Modelmaker)
Model Solutions

'Silk ...' 'Cut ...' Then let your
imagination fly. The ticker tape parade
uses 8ft high cheesegraters as
skyscrapers

Seibu (A) Hakuhodo, Tokyo
(AD) Takuya Onuki (CW) Naoya Okada
(P) Shintaro Shiratori

On March 11: the event at Kawasaki.
The opening of a department store in
one of Tokyo's most crowded and
polluted suburbs. Since becoming a
professional photographer, Shiratori has
never viewed reality as reality.

CHANGE THE SCRIPT

Pepsi (A) Abbott Mead Vickers BBDO, London (CD) David Abbott (AD) Greg Martin (CW) Pat Doherty (P) Mike Russell

Be prepared to meet the changes. The ad helps pave the way for Pepsi's new blue livery.

**DeBeers (A) J. Walter Thompson, Tokyo
(AD) Daishi Sumi (CW) Emiko Ura (Ps) Tetsuro Takai
(diamonds), Hiromasa Gamou (shell and dandelion)**

DeBeers created a series of cut diamonds to echo the patterns of nature. Charged with the task of promoting the variety of shapes, the creative team started with the premise that a diamond is a natural creation. From there it's a game of Pelmanism.

**Callithek/AquaLibra (A) Leagus Shafron
Davis Chick Ayer, London (AD) Mark Reddy
(CW) Richard Grisdale (P) Nick Georghiou**

Start re-arranging parts of the human
anatomy and let your imagination create
wild illusions.

The Finns invented the sauna (pronounced sow-na). They like to build them on the shores of their lakes, the idea being that nothing soothes the soul better than a period of total warmth followed by a moment of pristine, crystal-clear coolness. If you reverse this, you get the formula for Finlandia, which, as it happens, the Finns also invented.

Finlandia. Vodka From The Top Of The World.

**Heublein, Finlandia (A) Goodby Berlin
Silverstein, San Francisco (AD) Jeremy Postaer
(P) Duncan Sim**

The brief was to create an image that could be distilled in the bottle of vodka. It could be real. But the illusion was created using a chain saw, blow torches and black tarpaulin under six inches of water. The diver was photographed in London and added using a Quantel Paintbox.

Toyota (A) New Deal DDB Needham, Oslo (AD) Morten Foss
(CW) Steinar Borge

Don't worry if you're scared of something as highly technical
as a spanner. With this vehicle, you won't need one. What
would the company's founder, Kiichiro Toyoda, make of this?

Toyota RAV4

TOYOTA

Nostalgia

Virgin Megastore (A) BDDP, Paris
(AD) Eric Holden (CW) Rémy Noel (P) Jake

The past is no longer real. It is a fantasy,
relegated to the storyboard of our memories.

Shell (A) Bartle Bogle Hegarty, London

Reminiscent of the 'Go well. Go shell'
days of care-free motoring, the ads
rekindle a love of exploring car-free roads,
with the added mystery in the headline.

DISCOVER PARTS OF BRITAIN YOU NEVER KNEW EXISTED WITH SHELL.

Leave the A4 at Windsor and travel north on the old A355, guided by your free Shell maps.

Then it's headlong through the wooded heartland of Burnham Beeches, referring briefly to your Shell Illustrated Guide to Britain on Country Roads.

And choosing, on this occasion, to ignore the 100 castles, museums and theme parks, all of which are free to holders of Shell Explorer Passes.

Instead, it's onward, past the Post Office, deep into a maze of wooded lanes and the heart of Egypt, Buckinghamshire.

Join the Shell Explore Britain promotion today with this free starter voucher. Then collect the vouchers from participating Shell stations, for free maps, Explorer Passes and the Shell Guide to Britain on Country Roads.

YOU CAN TELL
WHEN IT'S SHELL.

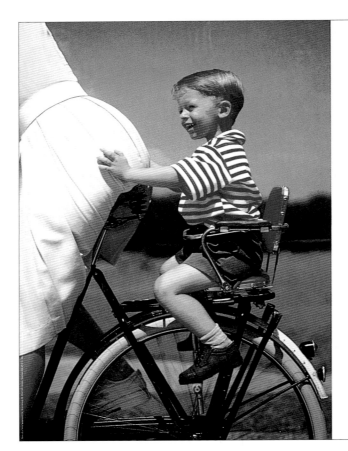

Dat veilige gevoel van vroeger.

Mercedes-Benz Nederland B.V.
(A) TBWA/Campaign Company, Amsterdam
(AD) Diederick Hillenius (CW) Poppe van
Pelt (P) Marcel van der Vlugt (main picture),
Paul Ruigrok (packshot)

Ah yes. I knew it reminded me of
something. Yesterday's safe feeling.

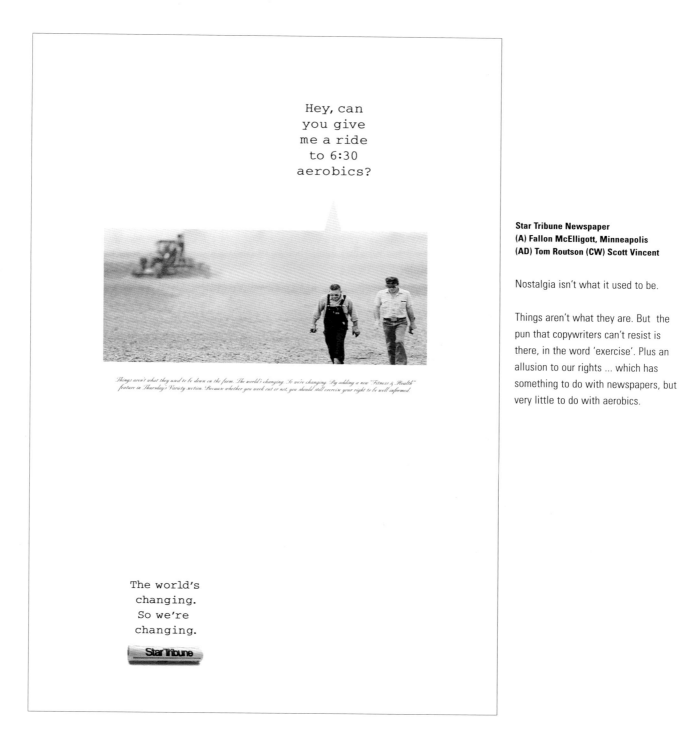

Hey, can
you give
me a ride
to 6:30
aerobics?

Things aren't what they used to be down on the farm. The world's changing. So we're changing. By adding a new "Fitness & Health"
feature in Thursday's Variety section. Because whether you work out or not, you should still exercise your right to be well informed.

The world's
changing.
So we're
changing.

Star Tribune

Star Tribune Newspaper
(A) Fallon McElligott, Minneapolis
(AD) Tom Routson (CW) Scott Vincent

Nostalgia isn't what it used to be.

Things aren't what they are. But the pun that copywriters can't resist is there, in the word 'exercise'. Plus an allusion to our rights ... which has something to do with newspapers, but very little to do with aerobics.

**Smirnoff/Moscow Mule (A) Lowe Howard-Spink, London
(AD/CW) Sue Higgs/Shay Reading (P) Stock Shots**

Take an idea, add a twist of ingenuity, a drop of humour and
mix with computer technology.
15% Judy Garland + 30% Marilyn Monroe + 15% Ingrid
Bergman + 40% Oliver Hardy = 100% original

If only I were Walter Mitty

Relax, the good feeling that nothing can disturb your peace of mind.

Even if a little accident should happen, as a customer of the "Zurich" you can breathe easily as soon as the first check is over. We'll take care of your problem quickly and unbureaucratically, as car-drivers who currently use our DRIVE IN damage service already know. So you can sit back and enjoy the comforting feeling that nobody understands you better than the "Zurich". That's Relax. But Relax also means: is there anything else we can do for you? Your customer representative has a few things on his hard deck and more than just insurance in his head. Because we at the "Zurich" want you to feel happy and well looked after. And we will do everything we can to achieve that. Call our HELP POINT line (freefone 0800 80 80 80) and talk to one of specialists who are there for you 24 hours a day.

ZURICH :relax

**Zurich Versicherungen/Relax, Dachmarke
(A) Wirz Werbeberatung, Zurich (CD) André Benker
(AD) Danielle Lanz (CW) Hans-Peter Schweizer (P) Peter Lavery**

Relax. However tricky or threatening the situation may seem, there's always a solution.

Nike (A) Simons Palmer Clemmow Johnson, London
(CDs) Andy McKay/Paul Hodgkinson
(AD) Glen Gibbons (CW) Simon Rosenblade
(P) Tim O'Sullivan, represented by Andrea Rosenberg

Launched in 1971, Nike was named after the Greek goddess
of victory. Now, if only...

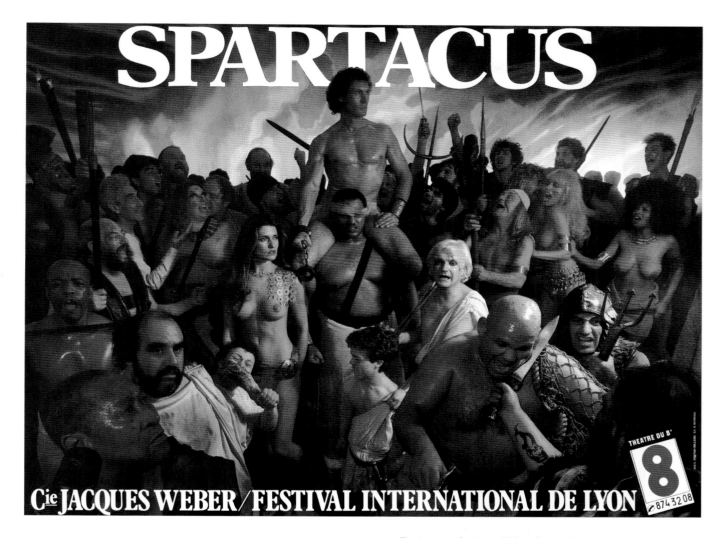

**Theatre poster Spartacus (A) Roux Seguela, Lyon
(AD) Beatrice Patrat (CW) Bernard Dufour-Mantel
(P) Michael Joseph (M) Tula/Caroline Cossey**

Despite the impression of movement, everyone
had to be well controlled as some 30 people
were crammed into an area of 12 x 20ft. By
moving an inch or two you might hide the
person behind or have a sword stuck in the
wrong place.

**Wilson (A) J. Walter Thompson, Tokyo (AD) Daishi Sumi
(CW) Yuko Ogita (P) Shinichi Kaneko**

Not satisfied with what you have at present? Win the game
with a dramatic solution.

知れば、必ず、欲しくなる。
想像を超える＋2.5cm。新開発フレームの
プロスタッフとハンマーにストレッチモデル、登場。
世界統一モデル、まもなく日本先行発売！

Teaser ads are not often used in Japan. The explosive entry of
the new, improved, 2.5cm longer version made quite a raquet

Swatch (A) Barbella Gagliardi Saffirio, Milan
(CD) Pasquale Barbella (AD) Franco Tassi
(CW) Roberta Sollazzi (P) Eugene Richards

While the world leaders get on with
important matters of state - such as
wearing a Swatch - others just watch.
Other brands are just watches.

**Ed. Abril/Revista Veja (A) ALMAP/BBDO, Sao Paulo
(ADs) Luiz Sanchez Jr & Rodrigo de Almeida (CWs) Tales Bahru &
Cassio Zanatta (Ps) Alexandre Catan & Arquivo de Imagem**

Do like a million subscribers: receive the world at your door.

Benetton (A) In-house, Italy (AD/P) Oliviero Toscani

In September 1995 the black man with different-coloured eyes became the symbol of Fabrica, a school dedicated to seeing into the future and challenging the boundaries of traditional communication through new art forms and new uses of technology.

**Liz Claiborne (A) Altschiller Reitzfeld
Tracy-Locke, New York (AD) Steve Mitsch**

REALITY IS THE BEST FANTASY OF ALL.

REALITIES

A FRAGRANCE FROM
Liz claiborne

ACKNOWLEDGMENTS

My thanks to all the humourously creative creatives whose work appears in this book. And to their PAs, secretaries and agents, as well as the art buyers and account handlers, who helped process the paperwork. Not forgetting the clients who commissioned the work in the first place.

My special thanks also go to Fran, Gromit, Penny Foulkes, Bob Prior, Tim Rich, Philip Spink and Wallace. To Claudia and Daniel for interior and jacket design respectively. And to Richard Reynolds whose velvet-coated brickbats have grown wings.

INDEX